T0002595

# Preparing the Way

Christian
Practices
for Advent

**the Way**

Scripture quotations are from the New Revised Standard
Version of the Bible, copyright ©1989 the National Council of
the Churches of Christ in the United States of America.

Psalm quotations are from the Book of Common Prayer.

#2671

ISBN: 978-0-88028-522-3

Library of Congress Control Number: 2023935676

© 2023 Forward Movement

Forward
Movement
inspire disciples. empower evangelists.

# Preparing the Way

Christian Practices for Advent

RICHELLE THOMPSON • LINDSAY BARRETT-ADLER
SCOTT GUNN • HUGO OLAIZ • MIRIAM MCKENNEY

Forward Movement

Cincinnati, Ohio

# Introduction

Wouldn't it be nice if stores had "Advent is coming" sales? They could have an endcap with wreaths and candles, some devotional books and journals and perhaps even purple or deep blue accessories. They could pipe in Advent music and dim the lights, inviting people to contemplate the holy in the weeks leading to Christmas.

Alas, Advent does not get much hype in stores—or in the secular world in general. Christmas decorations appear just as pools are closing for the summer. Hallmark and other TV and streaming channels start airing Christmas shows before Charlie Brown searches for the Great Pumpkin, and Mommy's kissing Santa Claus on the radio before the leaves hit the ground. It's hard to give Advent its due.

But the weeks leading up to Christmas should—and can—be sacred time. As we watch and wait for the birth of Christ, we have wonderful traditions such as the Advent wreath that can help us mark the time. Committing to worship each Sunday (and during the week, if possible) takes us on the journey with Zechariah, Sarah, and John the Baptist, then with Mary and Joseph (and Jesus!) as they make their way to Bethlehem. Many churches offer special services and activities that create space for reflection about what it means to welcome the Christ child.

At the same time, embracing Advent doesn't require us to wear earplugs and blinders, lest we accidentally engage in Christmas preparations. If we are intentional, we can infuse the holy into some secular traditions, from picking and decorating a tree to sending Christmas cards and celebrating the feast of Saint Nicholas. Most of us are not called to a monastic or hermetic life, set off from society. But Christianity has always been countercultural, from the moment the King of kings was born in a manger. We have the opportunity—and obligation—to let our faith play a role in all we do. These daily reflections written by the staff of Forward Movement offer insights, suggestions, and stories about ways to prepare our hearts and minds during the seasons of Advent and the 12 Days of Christmas.

During this time of year and always, let us bring glad tidings of great joy into our homes and communities, transforming our traditions with prayer, intention, and devotion.

Richelle Thompson
Editor, *Preparing the Way*

**A note:** We included a full four weeks of meditations for Advent. But the number of days in the season of Advent depends on the calendar. Feel free to skip ahead to Christmas Eve and Christmas Day (and, if you'd like, read the days you missed during the fourth week of Advent, too!).

# Getting ready

Almighty God, give us grace to cast away
the works of darkness, and put on the armor of light,
now in the time of this mortal life in which
your Son Jesus Christ came to visit us in great humility;
that in the last day, when he shall come again in his
glorious majesty to judge both the living and the dead,
we may rise to the life immortal; through him who lives
and reigns with you and the Holy Spirit,
one God, now and for ever. *Amen.*

—*The Book of Common Prayer*

The collect for the First Sunday of Advent sets the direction for the whole season of Advent. Many Anglican prayer books over the centuries have appointed this prayer to be said every day of the season. This prayer lays out a couple of key themes to help us savor these weeks leading up to Christmas.

As we pray, we are reminded that Jesus Christ will come again in glory, and we'd better be ready! That's an invitation to redirect our lives so that we are following Jesus in the fullest way we can. Whether we meet Jesus at his second coming or on the day we die, we will surely meet Jesus! And even if we focus on our earthly pilgrimage rather than its inevitable end, there's no downside to shaping our lives around our call as Christians. Advent is a wonderful season to think about meeting Jesus, whether we see him at Christmas or at another time.

The second theme of the collect has to do with light. The light of Christ is our armor. And, of course, the light of Christ is also a beacon that draws people to follow him. At this time of year, as the nights grow longer, light becomes a more powerful symbol. There's nothing like seeing the light from a single candle flame illuminate an entire dark room as a metaphor for the power of Christ's light to change our lives and our world. And if we use the light from one candle to light another, the light only magnifies. The first candle's light is not diminished when we light the second candle.

Of all the customs of this season, the Advent wreath is surely the most widely known. In an Advent wreath, there are four candles for each of the four weeks of Advent. At the start of Advent, one candle is lighted. On the second Sunday of Advent, the first and second candles are lighted. By the end of Advent, four candles burn brightly.

Over the course of Advent, as days become shorter and nights are longer, the Advent wreath burns more brightly. It's just like that with Jesus. When we need him most, there he is, offering the light of his grace and mercy.

Scott Gunn

## Going Deeper

If you don't have an Advent wreath at home, it's not too late. Maybe your church has the supplies to help you make your own wreath—or you can buy Advent wreath kits. But all you really need is four candles. At mealtime or when it's convenient, say a prayer and light the candles every day of Advent. As you light those candles and see how the light increases through the season, invite Christ to be your light.

# Counting the days

Our hearts are restless, until they can find rest in you.

—Saint Augustine of Hippo

Last year, my four-year-old daughter brought home an Advent calendar from her Philadelphia parochial school. I groaned as I unpacked it from her backpack; this would mark the fourth, yes the fourth, Advent calendar in our home. And it didn't even have chocolate! Perhaps sensing my disappointment and its future in the recycling bin, my daughter looked up at me and said, "When you open the door, there's the Bible!" I looked back at her and paused. I couldn't trash the Bible. So, we hung up our fourth Advent calendar and hoped the next one included candy.

As Advent unfolded, my daughter's words proved to be prophetic. Her calendar took us from the Annunciation all the way to Christ's birth and allowed us, as a family, to read pieces of scripture and journey together each morning. I now concede that her initial summary was correct—the whole arc of the narrative leads us to Christ. When you look in the manger on Christmas morning, there's the Bible.

From the initial joy of God's creation to the ways humanity continues to fall into sin and ruin, only to be redeemed by an ever forgiving and merciful God, scripture prepares us for the long and often frustrating wait for our savior. We identify with Israelites wandering through the deserts of our lives filled with confusion and doubt, we share the disbelief of Abraham and Sarah when God surprises and astounds us, we mourn with Martha and Mary when death comes for those we love, and we are drawn again and again to God's presence.

Advent calendars can be fun holiday decorations, filled with sweet treats and a physical countdown to Christmas morning. And also, with the turn of each small door, we can be reminded of the Biblical narratives and their characters who still ring true two millennia later. We wait and watch and pray and long for God's presence in our lives and our world. We look around us and, with every door that does not open to a manger scene, wonder, "How long, O Lord?"

Fourth-century saint, Augustine of Hippo, wrote in his *Confessions*, "You have made us for yourself, and our hearts are restless, until they can find rest in you." We are eager to get through this season of waiting for the Messiah. Turning each small door with Eve, Miriam, Elijah, Esther, Amos, Mary, Paul, Phoebe, and a great cloud of witnesses, we know that our redemption is at hand. We are restless to kneel before the manger.

Lindsay Barrett-Adler

## Going Deeper

Try including a sentence or two of scripture in this year's Advent calendar. Each day that you turn a door, read a passage and discuss it with friends or family.

# Service to others

In the biblical Advent story, we find inspiration to serve. In Luke's account of the nativity, the Virgin Mary chooses to call herself God's servant. "Here am I, the servant of the Lord", Mary replies when the angel Gabriel tells her that she will conceive and bear a son. "Let it be with me according to your word" (Luke 1:38). Later in the same chapter, Mary utters one of the most cherished poems of Christianity, the *Magnificat*, and again calls herself God's servant (Luke 1:48). In both instances, Luke uses the Greek word *doulē*, which can also be translated as "handmaiden" or even "slave."

Christmas and the weeks leading up to it are often touted as the season of giving—and rightly so. As Giving Tuesday approaches, many of us will receive dozens of requests from charities, nonprofits, and volunteer organizations (including our churches!) asking for a donation or a pledge. Seeing the ads on TV and social media platforms can be an overwhelming and even painful experience because we can feel that we are forced to make choices that dramatically affect people's lives.

During Advent, in addition to our church pledge, my husband and I typically donate to one or two organizations whose causes are close to our hearts. In the past, we have donated to Doctors Without Borders, to Episcopal Relief & Development, and to MOAS, an organization that has rescued thousands of migrants trying to cross the Mediterranean in improvised vessels. We pray our modest contributions join an ample pool of benefactors, which is how most nonprofits and volunteer organizations balance their books.

Yet there are other types of service that make this season meaningful: simple and unplanned acts of kindness that we can practice at the grocery store, in a parking lot, or at the airport. In one sense, these unplanned acts of service echo Mary's spontaneous response, "Let it be with me according to your word." They also recall the shepherds' speedy response found in Luke 2:15-16 to their angelic visitation: "When the angels had left them and gone into heaven, the shepherds said to one another, 'Let us go now to Bethlehem and see this thing that has taken place, which the Lord has made known to us.' So they went with haste and found Mary and Joseph, and the child lying in the manger."

Hugo Olaiz

## Going Deeper

How can Mary and the shepherds inspire you to make this Advent a season of service?

# Holy in the holly jolly

I want to be honest with you from the start: not all of our family traditions during this time of the year are focused on the divine. Elf on the Shelf? Yup. We did it. And it was fun for our two young ones and increasingly annoying for us as parents. On Christmas Eve, we threw out handfuls of oats and glitter for reindeer food, and one year, as our oldest started asking questions about Santa Claus, I made boot prints in the dust by the fireplace. She was mildly impressed but still skeptical.

It's easy to get sucked into the secular activities. Flashy gimmicks and a bevy of Pinterest pages spout the latest fads on how to bring the jingle-jangle into the season. That's why we try to balance the secular with the holy, practicing traditions that root us in the why of Advent and Christmas. For our family, celebrating the feast of Saint Nicholas has been one of the ways we call ourselves away from the holly jolly and into the holy.

On December 5, the evening before the feast of Saint Nicholas, our children set a pair of shoes on the fireplace hearth; in the morning, they received simple gifts: an orange, a bag of nuts, an ornament for the tree, and sometimes a pair of pajamas. They also received gold (chocolate) coins as a symbol of Nicholas's generosity. According to legend, Nicholas gave coins to a poor father to use for doweries for his daughters so they wouldn't be enslaved.

We talked about Saint Nicholas and the many legends surrounding his life. In addition to the stories about his secret gifts to help the poor and others, Nicholas is patron saint of sailors, reputedly calming stormy sea waters and saving travelers from death. These conversations rooted Santa Claus in the generosity of Saint Nicholas. When their young peers questioned the veracity of Santa, our kids would answer with stories about Nicholas. And interestingly, they seemed as excited to receive the simple gifts on the feast of Saint Nicholas as they were to open the latest tech gadgets on Christmas morning.

Our children are grown now, and our oldest is expecting her first. But they still set out their shoes and wake up to a handful of chocolate coins on the feast of Saint Nicholas. They—and we—are never too old to recall and honor the generosity of Nicholas the Wonderworker.

Richelle Thompson

## Going Deeper

Think about ways you can recover the historical Saint Nicholas. You might start the tradition of celebrating the feast day in your own home (whether or not you have children!). You could also follow in Nicholas's example and be generous in your gifts to children, especially the poor in your community.

# O Christmas tree

The tree tradition can be simultaneously full of fun and fraught. When do you buy a tree or get it out of storage? Do you prefer one color of light or multi-colored strands? Big lights or fairy lights? When do you decorate?

One thing I know about trees is that those who practice this tradition have a way. Our family has differing opinions, and our tree practices have evolved through our years together.

As a child, I don't remember having much say in how things happened. We had a formerly alive tree that we decorated with ornaments lovingly wrapped in tissue paper each year by my mom, who wrote notes on ornaments gifted to us. My parents kept everything, so we had an abundance of ornaments. We purchased our tree close to Christmas as my dad, an Episcopal priest, was a bit of a purist about Advent, and the tree was not a part of it. He was a fun dad, though, and gave in to my mom's desire to get the tree a little earlier.

I carried my childhood experiences into my family. For several years, my husband and I alternated spending the holidays with our parents. Then came a Christmas when we tried to go to Connecticut during a blizzard and had to turn around and come home, so we had our first Christmas by ourselves. We had an artificial tree back then because of our daughters' asthma. Then, one year, the girls clamored for a live tree. The next thing I knew, we had a new tradition of getting the tree on Thanksgiving weekend. "Hold on," I protested. "I don't want a tree this soon!"

"Mom," they said to me, exasperated, "the trees are scraggily when we wait until closer to Christmas." And did I mention these girls like trees that take over the living room? Meanwhile, I'm happy with a Charlie Brown tree that needs a little love. If it were up to me, I'd rent a tree in a pot and return it to rent again next year.

I have friends who planted an evergreen in their yard, and they decorate it every year as their offering to anyone who passes by. One of my dearest friends had a Christmas cactus that he kept up year-round decorated with fairy lights. My beloved neighbor, Joy, kept an artificial tree up all year, decorated with birds in nests with white ornaments.

Thinking of these loved ones and their tree practices as well as those of my family remind me that while the particulars seem essential and highly relevant at the moment, what matters most is your intention. Whatever you do with your tree—and when—matters as long as you're happy with it. For us, it's been lesson after lesson about compromise and making decisions together, which seems an appropriate way to move through the season of Advent.

Miriam McKenney

## Going Deeper

How can you be more intentional about decorating your tree—or house? In what ways can you make this a holy way to prepare for Christ?

# Christmas cards

I may be one of the last people who still sends snail-mail Christmas cards—and a robust letter—to friends, family, and parishioners. All together, we end up mailing about 400 cards each year. That's a lot of signing, stuffing, licking, addressing, and stamping. For a long time, I saw it as another chore on the never-ending Christmas to-do list.

But a few years ago, the task transformed for me into a holy time. The change began several months after Christmas when I received a note in the mail from a friend (who happened to be a priest, but her ordination status didn't necessarily play a role). She wrote that she had kept her Christmas cards, and each week, she pulled a couple from the stack. She committed to praying for the card's senders and writing a note to them, letting them know of her specific prayer intentions. It was a wonderful gift to know that my family and I were being prayed for by name, not because of a particular health concern, birthday, anniversary, or pending big decision, but simply because we were in relationship with one another.

The next Christmas, I decided to follow her example. Each week throughout the year, I randomly pulled four cards from the pile and wrote notes to let the senders know I was praying for them that week. I recalled a memory of our friendship or shared something that I admired about the person or had learned from them. This element gave me the opportunity to reflect on our connection and to give thanks for being in relationship with others.

An important component of this process was the random selection of cards. I wanted to give space for the Holy Spirit to work—and my goodness, did the Spirit show up! A few days after I sent one of the cards, I was in church when the recipient came up to me with tears in her eyes. "How did you know," she asked, "that the week had been so difficult? How did you know that I was in a dark place and needed a word of encouragement?" My answer was simple and honest: I didn't. But God did.

A few months later, I received a card in the mail from another person. She explained she felt bad about an incident that occurred twenty years earlier. She regretted her actions, and they gnawed at her, but she hadn't known how to reach out and apologize. She said that receiving the post-Christmas card note empowered her to forgive herself and to ask for forgiveness—and to realize that the relationship was far more important than any single event. To be honest, I didn't even remember what she was talking about, but it had weighed heavy on her heart. Thank God for the intercession of the Spirit.

I have tried to augment this post-Christmas practice with a pre-Christmas intention. When I address each card, I take a moment to thank God for the recipients. And when I receive Christmas cards, I hang them on my walls, where they stay through Epiphany. Each time I walk by, I'm reminded of the community of living saints who enrich my life in so many ways, and by word and example, shine the light of Christ into the world.

Richelle Thompson

## Going Deeper

Spend time thinking about ways that the tradition of sending Christmas cards can become a spiritual practice. If you're not a card writer or sender, think about another chore that you can transform into holy work.

# Go out to meet him

I look from afar and lo, I see the power of God
coming and a cloud covering the whole earth.

Go ye out to meet him and say: tell us, art thou he that
should come to reign over thy people Israel?
High and low, rich and poor, one with another,
go ye out to meet him and say: hear, O thou shepherd of
Israel, thou that leadest Joseph like a sheep.
Stir up thy strength, O Lord, and come to reign
over thy people Israel. Gloria Patri.

I look from afar…

— Advent Matins Responsory
*Saint Augustine's Prayer Book*

## Going Deeper

How are you preparing your heart to meet Jesus? Be
intentional in your spiritual practices this season.

# Brood of vipers

I am the voice of one crying out in the desert,
"Make straight the way of the Lord,"
as the prophet Isaiah said.

—John 1:23

The second Sunday in Advent usually introduces one of my favorite biblical characters: John the Baptist. He is blunt, abrasive, uncompromising, and deeply upset with the state of the world. Relying on language I use to describe energy levels with my two small daughters, John the Baptist is always at a 10; he is fired up and ready to go. Absolutely everything about John the Baptist is contrary to societal norms. He dresses himself in camel hair, eats bugs, lives in the middle of the desert, rants about repentance, and has no interest in worldly accolades. He is always the most offensive person in the room. Why, then is he one of my favorite characters?

I appreciate John the Baptist's unwavering focus on his ministry. He simply does not have time to worry about his outward appearance, popularity, or even diet. He will not dilute his message to make it more approachable or compromise his values in the face of disagreement. He does not worry about bruised egos or bending the knee. A prophet in the truest sense, he understands that he has a short window of time to communicate just how massively everyone has messed up and how important Jesus is in setting things right once again. From the very beginning of his documented life, John the Baptist is in action. He literally leaps in the womb with excitement for the Messiah and the deliverance he knows has finally arrived.

We can all learn many lessons from John the Baptist, but I try to recall his urgency for justice each Advent. So often people of faith talk about being prophetic, but what happens when our actions are put side to side with someone like John the Baptist? Do our words from pulpits and lecterns, our social media shares, or our annual service days alleviate societal injustice? Are we being so disruptive with our actions that proponents of the sinful status quo wish us dead and plot to do us harm?

John the Baptist does not have time for our self-delusion or inflated sense of importance. We are a brood of vipers who need to repent. As John the Baptist enters the Advent narrative, I hope we will all understand how important it is to focus on our ministries at hand. Mute all the worldly, prideful noise and repent of all the ways we harm ourselves and others by turning from God time and time again.

Lindsay Barrett-Adler

## Going Deeper

Prayerfully consider talking with your priest about confession this Advent season. In the Episcopal tradition, we commonly say, "All may, some should, none must."

# Simple gifts

The tradition of exchanging gifts during Advent and Christmas varies widely around the world. In many Latin American countries, children wait until Epiphany (January 6) to receive their gifts. These presents are a reminder of the journey of the magi, who after an unfortunate encounter with King Herod, were guided to Bethlehem by a star and gave their presents (gold, frankincense, and myrrh) to the Child (Matthew 2:1-12).

The adoration of the magi must have been very different from the Black Friday rushes that we have all seen on TV. Those spectacles, which occasionally include stampedes or riots, signal our tragic detour. Just like the magi, we have taken the wrong turn. In our quest to celebrate the birth of Jesus, we end up at Herod's golden throne.

For the past couple of years my husband and I have participated in a Secret Santa tradition with my brother-in-law's family. Each person is assigned at random another family member and tasked to create a gift with a monetary limit of about $10. Handcrafts and gift certificates for things such as "making your favorite dinner" are strongly encouraged. Above all, the Secret Santa exchange requires preparation; it invites us to think long and hard about the recipient and what they really like. The Secret Santa gift is not the only present our nephews receive for Christmas, yet with this simple tradition, their parents are helping them focus on what really matters. Although not a religious family, my in-laws are succeeding in an area where many Christians fail: they are teaching their children how to humbly follow the Star.

Last Christmas, my husband and I, along with my brother-in-law, his wife, their two sons, and our dog, Percy, sat again around the Christmas tree to open presents. When the time came to exchange the Secret Santa gifts, my nephew Balin, 11, was excited to give me a framed poem titled "The Adventure of Percy the Pernicious," which he had written and illustrated. Balin stood up, asked for silence, and proceeded to recite the poem. The first lines read:

> There was once a dog named
> Percy the Pernicious
> Who thought water bottles were delicious.
> Paper and magazines and cardboard
> she'd munch
> And jump on the table to eat Hugo's lunch.

My nephew Balin knows how much I love poetry, and how much I love our dog. With wild imagination (and probably some encouragement from his mom) he managed to create a unique, original gift that I will cherish forever.

Hugo Olaiz

## Going Deeper

Here are some suggestions for staying focused on the Star:

Consider limiting gifts to ones that are practical. Many adults nowadays admit that their perfect Christmas gift is a pair of warm socks! A popular meme on social media shows "the Three Wise Women" who arrive at the manger after the Wise Men to deliver fresh diapers, casseroles, and baby formula—the kind of gifts a newborn actually needs.

Look for service and volunteering opportunities during this season. You might do this as a family or even as part of a congregation-wide event. For instance, some churches start planning in Advent for participation in "Christmas in April." This one-day event is held on the last Saturday in April and sponsored by a non-denominational volunteer organization that repairs the homes of senior citizens who are low-income or physically challenged. For more information, visit ChristmasInAprilPG.org.

Some families bypass a traditional Christmas altogether and go on vacation instead. Some visit regions or countries that are warm during December and spend time as a family hiking, swimming, and learning about other cultures. A simple dinner in a remote place could make your Christmas all the more memorable.

Tuesday
The Second Week of Advent

# The Manger

I want to do something that will recall the memory of
that Child who was born in Bethlehem, to see with
bodily eyes the inconveniences of his infancy, how he lay
in the manger, and how the ox and ass stood by.

—Saint Francis as recounted by Saint Bonaventure

This Christmas Eve is the 800-year anniversary of the
first live recreation of the nativity scene. On Christmas
Eve in 1223, Saint Francis is said to have held a special
service inside a cave in Italy with a feeding trough as
manger surrounded by an ox and donkey. His friend and
contemporary, Saint Bonaventure, described the service
in his biography of Saint Francis: "The man of God stood
before the manger, full of devotion and piety, bathed in
tears and radiant with joy; the Holy Gospel was chanted
by Francis, the Levite of Christ. Then he preached to the
people around the nativity of the poor King; and being
unable to utter His name for the tenderness of His love, He
called Him the Babe of Bethlehem."

I have at least 35 nativity sets. There's the traditional
olive wood carving bought on a trip to Jerusalem, and a

beautiful porcelain Lenox set gifted piece by piece over several years from my mother-in-law. My father brought a stone creche back from Africa, and there's a dime-store plastic nativity from the 1950s that amazingly still winds and turns in circles.

Perhaps my favorite came, ironically, from Hallmark. The white ceramic tableau features young children putting on a Christmas pageant. The shepherd's crook and angel's wings are askew, a pageant director peeks around the curtains to see what disaster looms, and a young boy perches on a ladder to get a better look at the action. At the center of it all is the babe in a manger.

Eight-hundred years ago, Saint Francis tried to tell us this. In that first live nativity, Francis was bathed in tears and radiant in joy as he looked upon the reenactment of the birth of Christ. As we view various nativities today, set up in our houses and churches, whether olive wood or glass or papier mache or live reenactments, may we rejoice at the "Babe of Bethelehem," the incarnate God of love and light.

Richelle Thompson

## Going Deeper

As you view various nativities this season, think of the experience of Saint Francis and his response. How can these nativities help you prepare your heart for the coming of Christ?

# Saint Lucia

> Then in our winter gloom candlelight fills the room.
>
> —"Santa Lucia," Neapolitan folk tune

As we approached the holiday season in 2020, it became clear that our traditions of big family meals and gathering with people from multiple states would not be possible because of COVID-19 restrictions. If we hosted anyone from out of state or traveled to another state, we would need to quarantine for two weeks. Health officials encouraged everyone to limit their gatherings to 10 people or less, ideally from the same household.

Disappointed yet thankful that our family was healthy and not high risk, we decided to forgo hosting or traveling for the holidays. At the same time, we did not want our young daughters to miss out on holiday magic and memories. We made a list of all the feast days in Advent and Christmas (all twelve days!). Among other new celebrations was December 13, the feast of Saint Lucia.

Lucia was born in Italy in the third century and martyred for her public faith. Somehow her story made its way to

Sweden, and legends arose that she brought food to the hungry during a terrible famine. Often pictured wearing a wreath of lingonberry leaves and candles, Lucia also came to symbolize lightness in the darkest days of winter.

With our Swedish roots, we decided to incorporate these Scandinavian traditions into our Advent season. The oldest daughter is traditionally chosen to be Lucia, and a mom from our pandemic pod made our daughter a felt wreath headband complete with little felt candles. We enjoyed Lucia buns and Swedish cookies called *pepparkakor* and laughed together that her son refused to wear another traditional outfit, that of the "starboy."

As the adults sipped their coffee and our children ran around the living room with sticky hands, I found a moment of pure joy in the midst of that time of sorrow, loss, and uncertainty. This Advent would not feature holiday shows in packed school auditoriums, pews full of families worshiping together in church, or multiple generations enjoying dinner together. But lightness still cut through the darkness. Hope still prevailed. Love still reigned. God's light could not be hidden under a bushel or stamped out by despair.

Future Advents will find us in different circumstances and a global pandemic might not be the reason for our despair, but the forces of this world will always fight Christ entering the world. As we continue to journey through Advent, I am reminded of Lucia and the darkest nights that threaten to overwhelm us. Like Lucia and the traditional African American spiritual remind us, "Keep your lamps trimmed and burning, the time is drawing nigh."

Lindsay Barrett-Adler

## Going Deeper

In the midst of the world's struggles, where do you find hope, love, and reassurance? Light a candle and say a prayer of thanksgiving to God for these gifts.

# Armor of light

Almighty God,
give us grace to cast away
the works of darkness,
and put on the armor of light,
now in the time of this mortal life
in which your Son Jesus Christ
came to visit us in great humility;
that in the last day,
when he shall come again
in his glorious majesty
to judge both the living and the dead,
we may rise to the life immortal.
*Amen.*

—*Prayers New & Old*

## Going Deeper

Eat your evening meal by candlelight. Reflect on its glow.
What do you think the prayer means by the phrase,
"armor of light?"

# Soulful celebration

Many of the elements of Christmas tap me right into the past: trees, gifts, food, music, and Jesus. I have lots of favorites and have a hard time choosing one. My favorite Christmas cookie? Shortbread, sugar, and linzer. Favorite ornament? The angel with my name on it, the dove, no wait—the ones the girls made in preschool. Favorite creche? The portable one from African Team Ministries.

The one place I have no trouble choosing a favorite is Christmas music. I was a singer and sang in my high school choir and ensemble. We sang the "Hallelujah Chorus" from Handel's *Messiah* every year at our winter concert. I love singing it; I'm an alto and love that part. It's such a memorable piece that singers tend not to forget. Even years later, we can sing our parts.

On New Year's Day in 1993, I moved to New Jersey to be near my now husband. I was excited to start our life together and devastated to say goodbye to my job at the Undergraduate Library and my friends in Ann Arbor, Michigan. Those first three weeks were the worst. I had never felt so alone and far away before. I had to find a job, so I couldn't wallow. But I felt myself sinking.

As usual, music came to my rescue. A new Christmas album came out the year before called *Handel's Messiah: A Soulful Celebration.* I typically do not like remakes. They must be excellent for me to choose remakes over the originals. But a lot of my favorite artists were on this album, including incredible gospel singers. And Quincy Jones was on the album. I had to check it out. Thank God I did because that music saved my life.

What this album means to me—yes, the entire album— is that God answers us when we call. God hears us. God makes promises to God's people, and God fulfills those promises. All the songs kept their familiar structure but were arranged for solo or choral voices and used contemporary and traditional instruments. The words are all the same because they are from scripture. These songs were old friends. Hearing them in a new way gave me a reason to push myself out of bed every morning. I listened to the CD nonstop. The melodies and voices grooved into my heart.

My parents nurtured and cultivated my love for music. I took that love and used it to heal myself during a difficult time. *Handel's Messiah: A Soulful Celebration* is one of my family's favorite Christmas albums. While they don't love it as much as I do, we don't celebrate Christmas without it. All of the hope and joy I have in my life comes from God, and I'm thankful for gifted musicians who give me such a beautiful way to remember God's words.

Miriam McKenney

## Going Deeper

What Christmas music soothes your soul? Find some of your old favorites—online or on vinyl—and pray with them. You might even look for *Handel's Messiah: A Soulful Celebration*. Perhaps it'll become one of your favorites, too.

# Las Posadas

The *Posadas* (Spanish for inn, lodging, or shelter) is an Advent candlelight procession and celebration. In Mexico and some parts of Central America, it is traditional to hold Posadas during the nine days before Christmas, beginning December 16 and ending December 24. Through song, the Posadas reenact Mary and Joseph's long, frustrating search for a place where Jesus could be born. This tradition retells the story from Luke 2:1-7—but with a twist: at the end of the song, instead of rejecting them, the "innkeeper" welcomes Mary and Joseph into the home.

I grew up in Argentina—far away from the countries that celebrate Posadas. I experienced my first Posada in 1999, at a time when my spouse, who is Anglo, and I were worshiping with a predominantly Mexican congregation in Salt Lake City. Three years later, we invited our friends from that church for the first Posada we ever held in our home. I loved the opportunity to welcome our friends, and I felt that the message of the Posadas is simple yet powerful: by welcoming the poor and the needy, as with Joseph and Mary, we are welcoming Jesus into our midst.

This Advent, I challenge you to get involved in a Posada. It does not have to be a big production, and it does not have to be repeated for nine days. In the United States, a growing number of congregations, both Latino and Anglo, are adapting the tradition of the Posadas into a one-night event. The whole congregation, as well as neighbors and friends, are invited to participate.

Some people wonder whether it is acceptable for non-Latinos to appropriate this tradition. Based on my own experience, my answer is a resounding yes. The Posadas are, above all, a cultural tradition. Latinos are overwhelmingly pleased to see white Americans adopt and adapt traditional Posadas. At the end of the Posada song, it is not only Joseph and Mary but also all the pilgrims who are invited into the inn. This, it seems to me, points to a profound theological reality: whether Galileans or Judeans, whether Anglos, Latinos, or anything in between, we are all in this journey together, following the same Jesus.

Hugo Olaiz

## Going Deeper

Here are three ways you might participate in a Posada:

    1. Go to a Posada celebrated by a local church. Offer to bring your guitar and help play the song, dress up (you

and your children) as angels or shepherds, or help with the food.

2. Organize a Posada in your own church. Visit VenAdelante.org/posadas to find everything you need to host your own Posada, including a complimentary guide geared toward congregations, YouTube and MP3 versions of the Posadas song, and links to a Facebook page where people and churches post pictures and videos of their own Posadas. Produced by Forward Movement, these materials are free of charge in both English and Spanish.

3. Organize your own home Posadas! The guide at VenAdelante.org/posadas can be easily adapted to a home setting. Invite one or two more families to celebrate with you. Have the children learn the Posadas song beforehand, and ask them to make a piñata.

(Note: In recent years, some churches have felt moved to include in their Posadas explicit references to today's migrants and refugees. This is by no means required, but if you wish to explore this theme, Episcopal Migration Ministries has recently developed a resource that can be accessed at this link: VenAdelante.org/EMMposadas.)

Above all, relax! If this is your first Posada, start small. Ask for advice from Latino friends, but remember there is no wrong way to celebrate Posadas. Enjoy the opportunity to spend time with friends and family sharing a meal and remembering that we are joyfully awaiting the birth of Jesus.

Sunday
The Third Week of Advent

# Gaudete Sunday

Another Sunday, another candle in the Advent wreath. But this Sunday is a particularly special one. Many Advent wreaths, especially in Episcopal churches, have three purple (or deep blue) candles, to be lit on the first, second, and fourth Sundays of Advent. Today, on the third Sunday, we light the rose candle.

Traditionally, the third Sunday in Advent is known as Gaudete Sunday (or Rose Sunday). The name comes from the psalms, "Rejoice in the Lord;" *gaudete* is the Latin word for rejoice. While it seems like every Sunday in Advent should be a Gaudete Sunday—after all, we have much for which to rejoice—Advent is a time of introspection, of preparing our hearts for the coming of Christ. This introspection need not be dreary, but it should be thoughtful and intentional.

On the third Sunday, we get a reprieve, a lightening of this serious heartwork. It is a hinge of sorts as we move from the more somber and penitential scripture readings to the joy of the coming Christmas celebration. In most years in the liturgical cycle, we rejoice with the reading of the *Magnificat*, Mary's response to the angel Gabriel as she proclaims the greatness of the Lord.

Interestingly, rejoicing is not a request in scripture, but a command. "Rejoice always" we hear in 1 Thessalonians. This command kicks off a list of other exhortations—to pray without ceasing, to give thanks in all circumstances—all commands to live in ways that please God. And when we do, we find joy, even in the midst of sorrow or loss. We rejoice in God's promises made flesh in the form of Christ Jesus, born again and again in our hearts and lives.

Richelle Thompson

## Going Deeper

Wear something rose colored today as a reminder to rejoice always.

# Lessons and Carols

> Tears and smiles like us he knew;
> And he feeleth for our sadness,
> And he shareth in our gladness.
>
> — "Once in Royal David's City"

"Do you want to go to Lessons and Carols with me?" This, my friends, is how seminarians ask each other out on dates. Growing up, Lessons and Carols was not part of my Midwest, Lutheran household's Advent traditions. We had an Advent wreath, we sang about lighting candles to watch for Messiah, but Lessons and Carols? Huh? My then-boyfriend assured me there would be pretty music and, if nothing else, a reception afterward. Spoiler alert: that boyfriend is now my husband, and Lessons and Carols has become an Advent tradition I look forward to each year.

Each Christmas Eve morning, we tune into Minnesota Public Radio to hear the BBC broadcast of "A Festival of Nine Lessons and Carols" from King's College. As we welcomed one, and then two, and then three children, our Christmas Eve mornings became a little bit more hectic, but this morning broadcast remains an important Advent tradition for our family. Our kids know that the descant of "Once in Royal David's City" means Christmas is just one sleep away. Sometimes we enjoy a throwback radio show, listening together as a family in the living room, the kids playing and their tired parents enjoying cups of coffee. Sometimes Christmas is rushing toward us, and we listen in the kitchen, putting final touches on a Christmas cheesecake or placing the last cookie on the rack to cool. We have listened in the dining room, hard at work on gingerbread creations, and we listened when COVID restricted the number of people who could worship together in person.

This past year, we decided to bundle up the entire family (children ages 6, 4, and less than 1 year old) and join a local Episcopal congregation for Lessons and Carols. At the end of the service, our oldest daughter turned to me and said, "Mom, this is so much better in real life."

Lessons and Carols invites us to remember the redemptive acts of God through scripture and song, but God's salvation is so much better in real life. Christ's incarnation means God is with us, physically with us, to heal us with a touch and break bread with us at a table. God enters our very real, very messy, very broken world and offers salvation and restoration beyond our imagination. All of that awaits, but for now, "Once in royal David's city…"

Lindsay Barrett-Adler

## Going Deeper

If you attend Lessons and Carols in-person, invite a friend to join you this year. If you don't have a service nearby, tune into a radio broadcast Christmas Eve morning.

# O Antiphons

This litany is based on the Antiphons (refrains) appointed to be sung with the Magnificat at Evensong in the last few days of Advent. They are also the basis of the familiar hymn, "O Come, O Come, Emmanuel."

O wisdom, proceeding from the Most High,
reaching from one end to another,
mightly and sweetly ordering all things:
Come and teach us the way of understanding.

O Adonai and Leader of the House of Israel,
who appeared to Moses in the burning bush
and on Mount Sinai gave the Law:
Come to deliver us with your strong arm.

O Root of Jesse, given as a sign for all peoples,
in whose presence kings are silenced
and before whom all nations will be judged:
Come with the day of peace and do not delay.

O Key of David, who opens and none can shut,
leading us to life everlasting:
Come and lead out those bound in chains.

O Day Spring, the bright and morning star,
the eternal light that enlightens all:
Come and shine on those who sit in darkness
and the shadow of death.

O King of the Nations,
chosen and precious cornerstone,
binding in one all peoples:
Come quiet the strife that afflicts your children.

O Emmanuel, the promise
and the fulfillment of all promises:
Come and bring among us the joy of your kingdom.

Even so, Lord Jesus, quickly come.

*Amen.*

—*Saint Augustine's Prayer Book*

## Going Deeper

Some churches hold daily services, with a focus on each
of the O Antiphons. Consider attending one or more.
Focus on the different names of Jesus.

# Greening the church

Within the Episcopal liturgy, our senses are fully engaged: we hear the Word spoken and sung and the chime of *Sanctus* bells. We see light shimmer through stained glass and smell the woody notes of incense. Our hands warm with a greeting during the passing of the peace, and we taste the bread and wine as we gather at the table.

The tradition of "greening the church" is another feast of the senses. Many Episcopal congregations set aside a special time to decorate the churches for Advent and Christmas. Often, these decorations feature evergreens such as holly, pine, and fir, which retain their color even in the dead of winter. Their "ever-greenness" serves as a symbol of everlasting life through Jesus Christ.

In one of the congregations my husband served, a special greening of the church was held on the last Sunday before Christmas. After worship, most of the members stayed to help prepare the worship space. They hoisted ladders and hung evergreen garland from the chandeliers; they crafted wreaths for the pulpit and doors and carefully arranged swags on window sills. The sharp, sweet smell of pine and fir filled the nave, and the green of the branches with pops of red from holly berries was a sight to see. But for me, the sense most engaged in this tradition was sound: specifically, the buzz of a vacuum.

Those beautiful boughs have needles. And those needles like to fall. And somehow when they land on the ground, they form a death-grip on the carpet second only to Gorilla Glue. And so the vacuum was an essential tool in the greening of the church. While others decorated, faithful stewards took on the thankless job of vacuuming. They swept with a stiff-bristled broom, plucked out stubborn needles by hand, and then vacuumed again. And again.

Many of our essays in this book explore how to prepare our hearts and minds for Advent and Christmas. Most of the traditions are lovely or fun or both. We prepare by singing favorite songs, picking out a family tree, giving and getting gifts, reading the stories of Mary and Joseph and giving thanks for their faithfulness. We haven't spent a lot of time talking about the unpleasant, unfun parts of preparation. Those pesky needles from the evergreens remind us that some of our preparations may be tedious or even hard. Perhaps in the examination of our hearts as we prepare for Christ's birth we'll have to face some difficult truths about ourselves. Perhaps we are not as loving as Christ commands. Perhaps we harbor grudges against others or act in selfish, greedy ways that harm friends and strangers alike. Perhaps we are so focused on the razzle-dazzle of Christmas that we forget what it's actually about.

For the sake of wordplay, let's call these discoveries "needlesome"—vexing attitudes that we need to face and fix. Prayer is a good place to start. That, and a good vacuum.

Richelle Thompson

## Going Deeper

As you worship in the coming days, think about how the liturgies engage your senses. What sights and sounds and smells are important in your faith? How does what you hear and touch affect your spiritual life?

Thursday
The Third Week of Advent

# Doubting Thomas

Then he said to Thomas, "Put your finger here,
and see my hands; and put out your hand,
and place it in my side;
do not doubt but believe."

—John 20:27

On December 21, the Church celebrates perhaps the most relatable of Christ's apostles: Saint Thomas. Fearfully gathered in the days after Christ's crucifixion, the disciples encounter the resurrected Jesus and their faith is restored. Well, all except for Thomas. Unable to believe his friends, Thomas declares that he will not believe God overcame death until he sees the evidence in person. Jesus returns, provides Thomas his data, and then chastises him for his lack of faith.

Despite years of faithful ministry and eventual martyrdom, Saint Thomas will forever be known as "Doubting

Thomas." Modern people of faith might be quick to deride those who, like Thomas, find it hard to have faith in the unbelievable. We can almost hear someone we know saying, "Trust and have faith! Stop worrying so much about what will happen!" But if we are honest with ourselves, we can all identify with Saint Thomas and his feelings of uncertainty.

During Advent, we tend to focus on joyful themes like hope and expectation. But what of doubt? Think of all the moments of doubt that accompany the biblical characters journeying through Advent. Joseph is unsure if he should still marry his betrothed, Elizabeth and Zachariah wonder how they will take care of a child at their advanced ages, and Simeon is shocked into silence. No one anticipates God entering the world in poverty and persecution.

Like these familiar characters, we hear the promise of Christ's arrival throughout the Advent season. What awaits us is truly unbelievable, and we can be excused for having our doubts that the Messiah will come and set the world right. But, like Thomas, God does not leave us abandoned and alone with our feelings of doubt and despair. Christ returned to the room to show Thomas his hands, comfort his mourning friend, and remind him that death does not have the final word.

It is natural to have our doubts in a world so full of pain and injustice. Thank God we have a savior who meets us in our moments of doubt to provide reassurance and comfort. We are not abandoned in our questions and struggles but instead reassured that God knows our suffering and has come to show us resurrection hope.

Lindsay Barrett-Adler

## Going Deeper

What doubts do you have this Advent season? Begin cultivating a daily prayer practice where you sit with these doubts in God's presence.

# Montessori Christmas

On our way back to college, I told my youngest I was writing about a Godly Play Montessori Christmas. "What does that mean? Like how we live?" she asked. My oldest said the same thing. I can understand their question: how do you identify and describe something that seems like how we live?

Maria Montessori was an educator who believed in letting children lead their learning with direction and guidance from caring adults. This educational approach makes space for wonder. When our children were young, Christmas was indeed wonder-filled. However, one aspect of our Christmas celebration that made it different from other families is that we didn't do Santa. We decided we wanted to have a Christmas season focused on Jesus. We told our daughters that we were celebrating Jesus's birthday, and because Jesus lives in us, they got presents. We also said to them that there were children who did believe in Santa, and we did not want to change anyone's beliefs about Santa with our behavior.

Godly Play, a Montessori formation program, offers lessons about Jesus that create a mystery and wonder about him, and we extended that mystery into our Advent and Christmas seasons. Lots of kids love babies, so it was easy for us to get excited about a baby being born! Our children's ministry director was a very creative woman who made fabric ornaments as gifts for Sunday school teachers and helpers. One year, she made a candle, another year, a manger, another year, Mary, another year, a star. Even now, when my daughters decorate the tree, those ornaments are an invitation to talk about Christmases past.

The combination of our girls attending a Montessori school and a Montessori Sunday school meant that we live much of our lives in a Montessori way, which feels "normal" to us. My oldest daughter, Nia, said she appreciated the autonomy in all of our processes. The Montessori way empowers children to do things themselves, so we had dishes in drawers that our girls could reach. What they learned at school, we supported at home. They made gifts and ornaments and realized that a handmade gift could have a different value than a purchased one. We still have those ornaments made 25 years ago: pipe cleaner candy canes, paper snowflakes, glitter-covered Sweet Gum pods.

Nia said she appreciated clear communication about our Christmas seasons and the acceptance of questioning what was happening. Whatever we did, the girls were included and considered an essential part of the process. "Curiosity, wonder—these are welcomed in Godly Play and Montessori," Nia shared. "If I'm curious about a process, I'm safe to ask, and I'm confident in our definition of the narrative of Christmas. I'm not going to go to school and hate on someone else's wonderment if Santa really exists." Some kids wondered about Santa. We wondered about Jesus. And yes, we wondered about presents.

Miriam McKenney

## Going Deeper

What are your favorite traditions from childhood? How do they connect to your current Advent and Christmas practices? Talk to your family about these traditions. What new traditions can you change or create?

# Decorating the tree

Prepare the way, O Zion,
your Christ is drawing near!

—"Prepare the Way, O Zion"

Every Advent, my husband and I embody two beloved Christmas characters when it comes to decorating our home and Christmas tree. I like to imagine myself as Buddy the Elf, that lovable, joyful adult roaming around a big city in the movie, *Elf*. Buddy loves smiling, singing Christmas carols, and eating copious amounts of sugar. The day after Thanksgiving, I am ready to decorate the house, tune the car radio to the local holiday station, and put up our Christmas tree. I feel like I would be pals with Buddy the Elf.

My husband, channeling another beloved Christmas character, seems to look down from his mountain perch with a little dog beside him and mutter about those silly people with their silly tree, celebrating Christmas far too soon. A real Grinch. If it was up to my husband, our house would be bare of all Christmas tidings until after mass on Christmas Eve. You know, Christmas. As a middle ground, we put up our tree and other decorations the first Sunday in Advent.

In a way, our battle embodies major themes of Advent. My hope and excitement about Christ's arrival overflow. I cannot contain my yearning to unpack all of the adorable ornaments handmade by our children, those received as gifts early in our marriage, and those that adorned the trees of my childhood. The lighted star atop the tree reminds me to continue looking to the heavens for the Savior who has been promised. Decorating the tree, like a favorite hymn of mine, prepares our home for Christmas joy. Our Christ is drawing near.

At the same time, my husband reminds me that we are still very much living in Advent. A bright, beautiful, decorated tree shines in our living room, but the gifts do not arrive until Christmas morning. We can trim all the trees and deck all the halls as we prepare our hearts and homes for Christmas. But this Advent hope is nothing compared to the Christmas morning joy of our children rousing us awake before dawn yelling, "Wake up! Come downstairs! See what's under the tree!" Nestled under the tree full of decades of memories, are reminders of our family's blessings and love. My husband and I might disagree about decorations, but we both spend Advent in eager anticipation for the best gift ever given: God's only son and our savior. Maybe there is room for Buddy the Elf and the Grinch in Advent.

Lindsay Barrett-Adler

## Going Deeper

What are some of your favorite Christmas tree ornaments? Why are they so special and what memories are connected to them?

# Be not afraid

What would it be like to be visited by God every day? The collect for the fourth Sunday of Advent asks: "Purify our conscience, Almighty God, by your daily visitation, that your Son Jesus Christ, at his coming, may find in us a mansion prepared for himself" (The Book of Common Prayer, p. 212). The King James Bible occasionally uses the word "visitation" to refer to a day when God will come in judgement and glory (Luke 19:44, 1 Peter 2:12), but this collect invokes a neighborly God who comes to see us every day—always!

The fourth week of Advent is different from all the other weeks of Advent because its length varies from year to year. It can be as many as six days or, as in 2023, as short as a single day. When we light the fourth candle of the wreath, we know that Christmas is around the corner.

In the Advent wreath, the fourth candle is sometimes called the "Angel's Candle" and is associated with peace. It reminds us of the message that the angel delivered to the shepherds: "Do not be afraid. I'm bringing you good news. Peace" (Luke 2:10, 14).

If your Advents tend to be hectic, this last week may be the most hectic of them all. You may be consumed by preparations to travel or receive guests. The stores will likely be packed with shoppers and the freeways jammed with drivers. The weather could turn nasty. Airports can be madhouses. Everywhere, patience and civility will run thin.

As you prepare for Christmas, remember the words of the angel: "Do not be afraid. I'm bringing you good news. Peace."

Hugo Olaiz

## Going Deeper

This week, prepare yourself to be a mansion where Christ will dwell.

# Joyful thanksgiving

O Lord Jesus Christ, as you humbled yourself to
be born among us and laid in a manger, bring
us with the shepherds and wise men to kneel in awe
and joyful thanksgiving and to follow the steps of
your blessed life; that rejoicing now in your peace, we
may come at the last to eternal glory in your presence,
where the angels ever sing your praises. *Amen.*

—*Saint Augustine's Prayer Book*

## Going Deeper

Read up on the lives of shepherds in biblical times. Why
do you think God chose shepherds to be among the first
witnesses to Christ's birth?

# New way of living

Sometimes you see themes assigned to the four Sundays of Advent. It's pretty common to see Advent themes of love, joy, hope, and peace—or maybe those four words in a different order. But there is a more ancient set of themes for the four Sundays of Advent.

For hundreds of years, it was widely customary to encourage preachers to take up four themes on the four Sundays of Advent. These themes were death, judgment, hell, and heaven. This might strike us as a bit grim.

The truth is that we don't need to think of death, judgment, hell, or heaven as grim. Well, maybe hell is grim. But these themes invite us to take stock of our lives, to order ourselves so that we're always ready to meet Jesus Christ.

When I was a parish priest, I found the moments I spent with those who were contemplating death to be remarkably holy time. Sometimes I would be with grieving families, and other times, I was with people who knew they were nearing the end of their earthly pilgrimage.

In those moments, when death loomed large, all the distraction of life seemed to fade away to make room for the most important things. Material goods no longer mattered. Productivity at work didn't come up in these holy conversations. Instead, people who were facing their own death or the grappling with the death of a loved one always focused on love—love of God and love of neighbor.

One day, all of us will meet our maker. We will be judged. I'm not suggesting we should be scared into changing our lives. Rather, I'm suggesting that we are invited to change our lives. God's mercy is pure love, offered because God loves us.

In other words, don't be good just as fire insurance to stay out of hell. Rather, I think the reason to "be good" is to live righteously as God's prophets told us, as Jesus showed us, and as the Spirit leads us. Shaping our lives around love of God and love of neighbor is the best way to know the deepest joy of this life and to have hope for eternal joy in the life to come.

Scott Gunn

## Going Deeper

This Advent, if you run across themes of death, judgment, hell, and heaven, accept these final words as the beginning of a new way of living. As Christians, every day is a day to repent, to set our minds on Christ. This season of Advent is a wonderful time to get our bearings, to ponder our direction and our destination.

# Songs for the journey

Do you ever sing or hum while you walk? While you jog? While you run errands? In the Bible, singing is often associated with joyful journeys and particularly the return of Israelite exiles (see Isaiah 35:10 and 51:11). While in bondage, the people of Israel are too heartbroken to sing (Psalm 137), but on their way out of bondage, they sing, dance, and play tambourines, praising God for their liberation (Exodus 15:1-21).

When David brought the Ark of the Covenant back to Jerusalem, he "and all the house of Israel were dancing before the Lord with all their might, with songs and lyres and harps and tambourines and castanets and cymbals" (2 Samuel 6:15). There are reasons to believe that the pilgrims going to the temple sang joyful songs as well, as suggested in Psalm 138 and in Psalms 120-134, collectively known as "the Song of Ascent."

In Luke's account of the Nativity, the shepherds set out on the road to Bethlehem after hearing the angels praising God and "saying" (perhaps singing?): "Glory to God in the highest heaven, and on earth peace among those whom he favors!" (Luke 2:14)

Did that song kickstart the shepherds' journey? Is it possible they too sang as they approached the manger?

Coming from a culture that is familiar with religious pilgrimages and transnational migrations, Latinos sometimes see themselves as pilgrims, and some of the Latino Advent hymnody focuses on Mary and Joseph's journey to Bethlehem. Selections from the Latino hymnal *Flor y Canto* present this journey as hopeful and liberating:

Hymn #268 offers: "La Virgen sueña caminos, está a la espera; La Virgen sabe que el Niño está muy cerca." (The Virgin is dreaming of roads, she is in expectation; The Virgin knows that the Child is very close.)

And in Hymn #7, we hear: "Por la ruta de los pobres va María, va José; Van camino de Belén; En sus ojos mil estrellas, en su seno Emanuel." (Along the way of the poor, there goes Mary, there goes Joseph; They are on their way to Bethlehem; In their eyes, a thousand stars; in her bosom, Emmanuel.)

How would your Advent be different if you were to imagine yourself as Mary and Joseph's fellow traveler, with Bethlehem as your destination?

Hugo Olaiz

## Going Deeper

Consider starting a program of walking the dog, hiking, or even jogging as part of your daily routine. Sing or listen to Advent/Christmas songs while you exercise. In what other ways can you make songs and hymns part of the Advent journey?

# Splendor

Creator of the stars of night,
your people's everlasting light,
O Christ, Redeemer of us all,
we pray you hear us when we call.

In sorrow that the ancient curse
should doom to death a universe,
you came, O Savior, to set free
your own in glorious liberty.

When this old world drew on toward night,
you came; but not in splendor bright,
not as a monarch, but the child of Mary,
blameless mother mild.

At your great Name, O Jesus,
now all knees must bed, all hearts must bow:
all things on earth with one accord,
like those in heaven, shall call you Lord.

Come in your holy might, we pray,
redeem us for eternal day;
defend us while we dwell below
from all assaults of our dread foe.

To God the Father, God the Son,
and God the Spirit, Three in One,
praise, honor, might, and glory
be from age to age eternally.

Ninth-century hymn
*The Hymnal*, #60

## Going Deeper

Look through the Advent hymns on pages 53-67 of the
Episcopal Church's hymnal. Explore the lyrics in different
ways: pray with them, read as a poem, express the words
with art. And, of course, sing them!

# Songs of Christmas past

Grant us, Lord, not to be anxious about earthly things,
but to love things heavenly; and even now,
while we are placed among things that are passing away,
to hold fast to those that shall endure;
through Jesus Christ our Lord,
who lives and reigns with you and the Holy Spirit,
one God, for ever and ever. *Amen.*

—*The Book of Common Prayer,* p. 234

Do you listen to a specific set of songs or hymns during Advent and Christmas? Do they reflect a tradition received from your parents, or do they combine, in some way, the old and the new? Are you consciously trying to keep alive this tradition in your life, and perhaps even pass it on to your children?

Every Thanksgiving, as we head off to visit friends on the other side of the state in Cleveland, my husband and I take in the car a small CD wallet labeled "Xmas." Our Advent starts on the Sunday after Thanksgiving, during the ride back home, when we play songs from those CDs for the first time in the year. Our collection contains both secular and sacred music, Advent as well as Christmas songs. During our 5-hour ride, we typically hum or sing along with some of the hymns.

Despite being small and eclectic, our collection is very meaningful for us because it evokes friends, family, and memories of Christmas past—including memories that we built together. For example, the collection includes a Reader's Digest CD-ROM that was gifted to us by my mother-in-law before she passed from cancer. The song "Lo, How a Rose E'er Blooming" is full of happy memories for me because I first sang it during the same Advent that I started to date my husband. The most precious disc of the collection is a version of "Amahl and the Night Visitors" copied from an old VHS videocassette, with my husband (then age 10) singing the part of Amahl.

The collection also includes one Christmas song that evokes a very sad memory: my aunt Edith, whom I never met, died in a fiery motorcycle accident on Christmas 1963. When I was a child, the story of her passing was a taboo subject. During our Christmas celebrations, my grandmother stayed in her room, and my brother and I were instructed never to say "Merry Christmas" to her. Later, I learned the details of my aunt's accident from a newspaper clipping. The article mentioned Christmas records "melting by the heat of the fire." Since the family record collection included a rendition of "O Holy Night," which my parents never played, I assumed, perhaps mistakenly, that this record had survived the fire. Every time I hear "O Holy Night," I think of my aunt's tragic passing and my grandmother's endless mourning.

During Advent and Christmas, music can be a powerful tool to evoke memories. It can help us feel the season's spirit and "not to be anxious about earthly things." However, the purpose should not be to make us feel good or nostalgic only but also to inspire us to "hold fast to those [that] shall endure" and to help us build new memories and new traditions.

—Hugo Olaiz

## Going Deeper

What Advent and Christmas songs have special memories for you? Consider learning a new song and adding it to the repertoire.

## Saturday
## The Fourth Week of Advent

# Christmas Eve

Father, in this holy night your Son was born among us, and Christians all over the world sing for joy; renew your Church and open our hearts that Christ may find in us a dwelling place prepared for himself.

*Silence may follow each petition*

In this holy night, the angels sang of "Peace on earth and good will among men." We pray for the leaders of this country and all in authority, that they may work for peace and promote the well-being of all.

Lord, in your mercy, *hear our prayer.*

In this holy night, the shepherds found the Christ Child lying in a manger, with the Blessed Virgin Mary and Joseph; bless our homes and families, and all those we love.

Lord, in your mercy, *hear our prayer.*

The darkness of this night is scattered with the light of Christ's presence; bring comfort to all who suffer, who grieve, or who are alone. Lord, in your mercy, hear our prayer. In the word made flesh, you have joined heaven and earth; keep in safety all those who have died and bring us all to the joys of heaven.

Lord, in your mercy, *hear our prayer.*

—*Saint Augustine's Prayer Book*

## Going Deeper

Sometime today, set aside 10 minutes. Close your eyes. Turn off the TV and phones. Sit and listen. What is God saying to you?

Christmas Day

# Good tidings of great joy

But the angel said to them,
"Do not be afraid; for see—
I am bringing you good news of great joy
for all the people:
to you is born this day in the city of David
a Savior, who is the Messiah, the Lord.

—Luke 2:10-11

And I heard a loud voice from the throne saying,
"See, the home of God is among mortals.
He will dwell with them;
they will be his peoples,
and God himself will be with them."

—Revelation 21:3

## Going Deeper

Rejoice! Rejoice!

# Light and love

On June 16, 2022, a stranger walked into the Parish Hall of St. Stephen's Episcopal Church in Birmingham, Alabama. He carried a plate of shrimp and a flask. After so much time in isolation because of the pandemic, members of the "Boomers" group were excited to gather for their monthly potluck, and a couple of the members approached the stranger, welcoming him to the dinner and asking him to join their table. A few moments later, he opened fire, killing three beloved church members.

On this day, the wider church commemorates the feast of Saint Stephen, known as the first martyr of the church. The Book of Acts recounts how Stephen was one of the first deacons—those especially charged with caring for the poor, the needy, and the stranger. Stephen preached the Gospel of Jesus in word and deed, which angered the authorities of the day. Because of his faith, they stoned him to death.

In a sermon the Sunday after the shootings in Birmingham, St. Stephen's rector, John Burruss, spoke about the congregation's guiding principle of following Jesus's example of welcoming all to the table. Jesus even invited Judas to the table, Burruss preached, knowing that he would be betrayed but that love mattered more. There's no doubt, Burruss said, that the three slain parishioners of St. Stephen's would invite their Judas again and again to "sit at the table and share a meal because they knew God's unconditional love, and it was their guiding ethic. They fully embodied it. They knew it is the way to eternal life."

It's a powerful juxtaposition for us, having celebrated Christ's birth just yesterday and now remembering the violent death of Saint Stephen, who lived for Christ. If the story ended with the miraculous birth of Christ, it would be a beautiful, incredible tale indeed. But we know that birth is only part of the narrative. The real story—our Christian story—is a life and death and life one. It's a blockbuster beyond compare.

Sometimes martyrs and saints are people who lived and died long ago. And sometimes they are people in our midst, people so convicted by love of Christ that they extend a hand to a stranger. Thanks be to God for Saint Stephen and the saints of St. Stephen's. Amen.

—Richelle Thompson

## Going Deeper

The people of St. Stephen's Episcopal Church made a conscious decision after the gun violence to choose light, to choose grace and forgiveness and love. Are you struggling with a difficult situation, anger, or heartache? What steps can you take to make a conscious decision to choose light and life?

# Grace upon grace

Shed upon your Church, O Lord, the brightness of your
light, that we, being illumined by the teaching of your
apostle and evangelist John, may so walk in the light
of your truth, that at length we may attain to the
fullness of eternal life; through Jesus Christ our Lord,
who lives and reigns with you and the Holy Spirit,
one God, for ever and ever. *Amen.*

—*The Book of Common Prayer,* p. 238

If I could only take one chapter of the Bible to a desert
island to read every day, it would be the first chapter of
the Gospel of John. The poetry of this chapter is majestic.

*In the beginning was the Word, and the Word was with
God, and the Word was God. He was in the beginning
with God. All things came into being through him, and
without him not one thing came into being. What has come
into being in him was life, and the life was the light of all
people. The light shines in the darkness, and the darkness
did not overcome it.* (John 1:1-5)

Here, John explains how Christ was present from the
creation onward, offering the light of God's grace and

mercy to the world. If you haven't read it before, go grab a Bible or pull up Google and read John 1.

From ancient times, much of the church has commemorated John the Evangelist on December 27. He is author of the fourth Gospel, three short letters, and the Revelation. There is no widespread agreement on why today is the day we remember John, just two days after Christmas Day. I like to imagine that it is because he writes the poetry that tells us why we celebrate Christmas. Matthew and Luke tell us what happened, but John gives us the big picture, the why.

Whenever I'm asked about my favorite Bible verse, it's an easy choice. I love John 1:16. "From his fullness we have all received, grace upon grace." Jesus Christ's birth is not just a wondrous story—though it is that—but it is a manifestation of the Father's love for us. God sent his son into our world to save us. Jesus is pure glory, full of grace and truth. And God's loving gift of grace and truth is for all of us.

Scott Gunn

## Going Deeper

Today, give thanks for the witness of Saint John. Perhaps you'll honor Saint John today by reading part of his Gospel or one of his letters. And, above all, in this Christmas season, give thanks for the abounding grace to which Saint John pointed us.

# Justice, love, and peace

We remember today, O God,
the slaughter of the holy innocents
of Bethlehem by King Herod.
Receive, we pray,
into the arms of your mercy
all innocent victims;
and by your great might
frustrate the designs of evil tyrants
and establish your rule of justice, love, and peace;
through Jesus Christ our Lord,
who lives and reigns with you,
in the unity of the Holy Spirit,
one God, for ever and ever. *Amen.*

—*The Book of Common Prayer,* p. 238

The second chapter of Matthew tells us about a great calamity. Fearing the infant Jesus, King Herod ordered all the infant males in Bethlehem to be slaughtered. Because of his fear of one, he murdered many. Jesus was spared, because his family fled to Egypt as refugees, as Joseph had been warned in a dream that he was in danger.

It's horrific to contemplate. Deliberate murder is always terrible, but the murder of an innocent child is especially disturbing. The slaughter of many children is almost beyond comprehension.

This feast day commemorates not just those innocent babes who were murdered in Bethlehem, but all innocent victims. Each person is precious to God, and I can only imagine the great mercy God must show to those whose lives are ended so cruelly.

In the United States, I've not seen much emphasis on this horrific chapter in the Christmas story. Perhaps this is because we have distanced ourselves from death here. When I traveled in the Holy Land, I noticed that almost as popular as Nativity scenes, many places displayed carved figures of the Holy Family fleeing to Egypt. This part of the story looms larger there.

While I have no desire to rob anyone of their Christmas joy, I do hope we will not turn away from this awful reality.

It's easy to point our finger at King Herod as a monster. But what if we consider this feast day in its broader sense? As we remember all innocent victims, we might spend time thinking about who are today's innocent victims. It is deeply horrifying to realize how many children are hungry in this land of abundance. The number of children who die each year from gun violence is staggering.

As we remember the feast of the Holy Innocents, let us resolve to shape our world so that there are no holy innocents in our time. We cannot turn away from horror. Instead, we must gaze on what is amiss and repent of all that brings innocent people to harm.

Scott Gunn

## Going Deeper

As the prayer for today says, let us do our part to "frustrate the designs of evil tyrants and establish [God's] rule of justice, love, and peace."

December 29

# Twelve days of Christmas

> Joy to the world! the Lord is come.
>
> —"Joy to the World"

I have the following vivid memory of post-church Advent Sunday services growing up:

Child Lindsay: "When can we sing Christmas carols?! I want to sing CHRISTMAS carols!"

Priest Dad: "On Christmas. It's still Advent!"

The time has finally come! Break out the Christmas carols! Light the white candle! Move baby Jesus to the manger scene! MERRY CHRISTMAS!

In our culture, it has become customary to begin celebrating Christmas sometime around Halloween. Trees show up in stores, twinkling lights are hung above porches, and Santa begins posing for photos at the local mall. Perhaps the most interesting modern, cultural countdown to Christmas is a television channel's "25

Days of Christmas" lineup, chock full of holiday-themed entertainment. Talking with friends one year, everyone in the room was shocked to learn that the traditional Twelve Days of Christmas are celebrated after Christmas. Shock and horror filled faces and someone loudly proclaimed, "After?! But what's the point? By then, Christmas is over!"

Yes, December 26 does usher in a period of post-holiday malaise: our pants are a bit tighter; our bank accounts are a bit thinner, and our Christmas cheer is packed up with stockings and garland. But my friends, Christmas is not over! Christmas is just begun!

The twelve days of Christmas invite us to enter a joyful time of celebration and thanksgiving to God. In the next twelve days, traditionally known as Christmastide, we will commemorate saints Stephen and John, remember the Holy Innocents, and celebrate the Holy Name of Jesus. These twelve days are sandwiched between Advent and Epiphany, the time of expectant waiting and Christ's welcome to the entire world.

God has just become Emmanual, God with us. This is revolutionary. What if we spent the next twelve days truly celebrating and pondering the meaning of Christmas? Instead of packing everything up and moving on to Valentine's Day decorations, savor these twelve days and pack them full of Christmas traditions we are tempted to begin in Advent. Savor the carols and cookies; savor the tree's glow and glad tidings. In a world that simply cannot wait for anything, it is worth the wait when God changes everything.

Lindsay Barrett-Adler

## Going Deeper

Research the feast days that occur during Christmastide and choose one tradition to celebrate this year.

# O Little Town of Bethlehem

O little town of Bethlehem, how still we see thee lie!
Above thy deep and dreamless sleep the silent stars go by;
yet in thy dark streets shineth the everlasting Light;
the hopes and fears of all the years are met in thee tonight.

For Christ is born of Mary; and gathered all above,
while mortals sleep, the angels keep their watch of
wondering love. O morning stars, together proclaim
thy holy birth! And praises sing to God the King,
and peace to men on earth.

How silently, how silently, the wondrous gift is given!
So God imparts to human hearts the blessings of his
heaven. No ear may hear his coming, but in this world
of sin, where meek souls will receive him,
still the dear Christ enters in.

Where children pure and happy pray to the blessed Child,
where misery cries out to thee, Son of the mother mild;
where charity stands watching and faith holds wide the
door, the dark night wakes, the glory breaks,
and Christmas comes once more.

O holy Child of Bethlehem, descend to us, we pray;
cast out our sin and enter in, be born in us today.
We hear the Christmas angels the great glad tidings tell;
O come to us, abide with us, our Lord Emmanuel.

—Phillips Brooks
*The Hymnal*, #78

## Going Deeper

This beloved hymn was written by Phillips Brooks, an Episcopal priest who served as rector of Trinity Church in Boston. Inspired by a visit to Bethlehem in 1865, he wrote a poem for the church and asked his organist, Lewis Redner, to put it to music. Tonight or one evening in the coming days, go outside and look at the night sky. Recite the lyrics of this hymn, paying special attention to the stars. How can you, like the "morning stars" Brooks describes, proclaim Christ's holy birth?

# Sharing a meal

Isn't a meal together the most
beautiful expression of our desire
to be given to each other in our brokenness?
The table, the food, the drinks, the words, the stories:
Are they not the most intimate ways
in which we do not only express the desire
to give our lives to each other,
but also to do this in actuality?

—Henri Nouwen, *Life of the Beloved*

The gospels give us some intriguing glimpses of situations in which Jesus shared food and drink with others: Jesus dines with tax collectors and sinners (Mark 2:15, Luke 19:7); he receives water from a Samaritan woman (John 4:4-42); he meets a boy who shares five loaves and two fish (John 6:1-13). All these encounters, I believe, depict Jesus engaging with strangers or with people who were not like him.

In remembrance of Jesus's actions during the Last Supper, the early church gathered and "as they spent much time together in the temple, they broke bread at home and ate their food with glad and generous hearts" (Acts 2:46) and shared their food with the less fortunate (Acts 6:1-7). Although we tend to think of the eucharist as a merely symbolic meal, the account we find in 1 Corinthians 11 (and later, in the writings of Justin Martyr) does not describe a symbolic meal (a few crumbs of bread, a sip of wine) but a full meal. This meal, shared perhaps as a Sunday dinner, was at the very essence of what it meant to be a Christian.

When I lived in North Carolina, my husband and I attended a fledgling new congregation, The Church of the Advocate, in Chapel Hill. Every Sunday, after the service, we walked to the basement where we shared a dinner that the congregation described as "an extension of our eucharistic meal." This was a great opportunity to get to know the people with whom we worshiped. During those dinners, we learned about each other's lives and occasionally celebrated birthdays or baptisms. Since we met in a space owned by a kosher-observing Jewish congregation, the meals were simple vegetarian potlucks that often included rice, beans, or casseroles.

Christmas is a good season for fortuitous encounters. The Gospel of Luke describes a series of encounters in which a diverse group of people became part of a sacred story. These encounters can be as fleeting as Simeon's canticle (Luke 2:25-35) or the shepherds' visit to the manger (Luke 2:15-20).

We too are part of a sacred story. And just like the Holy Eucharist, our shared meal and interactions become "a foretaste of [God's] heavenly banquet" (The Book of Common Prayer, p. 482). We will share that wedding banquet with all the saints, forever, and none of us will ever be hungry or thirsty again.

—Hugo Olaiz

## Going Deeper

Share a meal with someone you don't know well—perhaps a neighbor, a coworker, or someone in your faith community. You could do something as a simple as sharing lunch in a quiet café or a simple dinner at your home. Even a cup of coffee would count. In fact, the simplicity of the meal could help you focus on the person instead of the food.

Another option is to volunteer in a soup kitchen or some other initiative to feed the hungry. Whatever you choose, make sure that the experience includes interactions with fellow volunteers and with the people you are serving.

## January 1

# Holy Name

Eternal Father, you gave to your incarnate Son
the holy name of Jesus to be the sign of our salvation:
Plant in every heart, we pray, the love of him
who is the Savior of the world, our Lord Jesus Christ;
who lives and reigns with you and the Holy Spirit,
one God, in glory everlasting. *Amen.*

—*The Book of Common Prayer,* p. 213

All names have power. When someone calls us by name, we listen. Most of us have names that were carefully chosen by others. Our names help define us. These things are true for Jesus, too.

But with Jesus, there's even more to his naming. Today, we celebrate the Holy Name, exactly eight days after Jesus's birth. It was the custom then that newborn boys would be taken eight days after their birth to be circumcised and to formally receive their name.

Of course, Jesus's name was given by God through an angel. While there is some scholarly disagreement about the exact meaning of "Jesus," many say that this holy name means "the Lord saves." His name defines him. He defines his name.

Jesus once said, "Very truly, I tell you, if you ask anything of the Father in my name, he will give it to you" (John 16:23). Jesus's name has power when we pray. That's why many of the prayers in the Book of Common Prayer are addressed to the Father and then conclude with "through Jesus Christ our Lord." When we pray like this, we are fulfilling Jesus's charge to us.

So today we focus on Jesus's name and its power. There is a danger that we become so familiar with the name of Jesus that we forget its power. Perhaps this is why the church has set aside this feast day every year for us to remember and treasure the power of Jesus's name. Throughout the year, to keep in mind the holiness of his name, many people bow their heads every time they hear the name of Jesus. Our bodies become reminders and teachers.

Scott Gunn

## Going Deeper

If today you invoke the holy name of Jesus, what will you ask?

# January 2

# **Blessed eternity**

O Lord God of time and eternity,
you make us creatures of time that,
when time is over, we may attain your blessed eternity:
With time, your gift, give us also wisdom
to redeem the time, lest our day of grace be lost. *Amen.*

—*Prayers for All Occasions*

## **Going Deeper**

Many people are making new year's resolutions. Do any
of your resolutions address your spiritual life? What can
you do to revel in this time given by God?

# Love came down

Starting in late autumn, many stores began to play Christmas music. And then right on schedule on December 26, they went back to their usual music and shut off the Christmas tunes. But there's another rhythm available to us.

Every year about this time, I'm enjoying my favorite Christmas songs. While I don't inflict my practice on others, I'm pretty strict about only listening to Advent music in the season of Advent. It's helpful to me to keep my mind focused on preparing for Christmas. And then, starting on Christmas Eve, I switch to Christmas music. And then that's all I listen to until January 6.

But not everyone needs to keep this rhythm. I know a friend who keeps Advent but who also plays Christmas carols in their home throughout December. How else, she reasons, will their children hear and learn Christmas music? By listening to Christmas music at home, the kids are ready to sing along when they come to church on Christmas.

My point is that there's no wrong or right way to listen to Christmas music. You can enjoy Christmas in July!

There's no downside to remembering the birth of Jesus any time. I do hope you find a way to listen to Christmas carols and hymns, and perhaps you will even sing along. So much beautiful truth is revealed for us in the ancient and modern music of Christmas.

For example, Christina Rossetti's "Love came down at Christmas" won't ever be a chart-topping single, but it is well worth singing and pondering.

> Love came down at Christmas,
> love all lovely, love divine;
> love was born at Christmas:
> star and angels gave the sign.
>
> Worship we the Godhead,
> love incarnate, love divine;
> worship we our Jesus,
> but wherewith for sacred sign?
>
> Love shall be our token;
> love be yours and love be mine;
> love to God and neighbor,
> love for plea and gift and sign.

This song reminds us that love is what Christmas is all about. By humming along, we can form ourselves to recall that Christ's birth is part of God's revelation and desire to save us. Jesus, as they say, is the reason for the season. And love is the reason for Jesus.

—Scott Gunn

## Going Deeper

What Christmas songs are special to you? Find a copy of the lyrics and use them in your prayers.

# Rising of the sun

I will give you as a light to the nations,
that my salvation may reach to the end of the earth.

—Isaiah 49:6b

For from the rising of the sun to its setting
my name is great among the nations, and in every place
incense is offered to my name, and a pure offering;
for my name is great among the nations,
says the Lord of hosts.

—Malachi 1:11

## Going Deeper

These words from Malachi call upon people to offer incense as praise to God. When you read scripture or pray, do you engage the sense of smell as well as your other senses? Consider lighting incense during your prayers. Or, cook an extra batch of your favorite meal and share it with a neighbor. Enjoy the smells as a reminder that you are the hands and feet of Christ in the world.

# Chalking the door

Epiphany is a spectacular feast, signaling the end of the season of Christmas with a commemoration of the visit of the three magi. The word epiphany comes from Greek and means to appear, and on this feast, we recall Jesus's manifestation—appearance—to the Gentiles. Presumably the shepherds and others who have seen Jesus, along with his parents, are Jews, and now, with the Epiphany, the Christ child appears as a light to all the world.

One way we can play a role in proclaiming that manifestation is by public affirmations of our faith. This includes acts of service, generosity in spirit, and sharing the Good News of the Gospel. A centuries-old Epiphany tradition can help. On or before Epiphany, many Christians "chalk the doors." They write a particular series of numbers and letters above the entrance of their home. Adapted for 2023, the writing would appear as: 20 + C + M + B + 23. The numbers signify the year (2023), while the letters represent the initials of the three wise men, Caspar,

Melchior, and Balthasar. They are also abbreviations of the Latin phrase, *Christus mansionem benedicat*, which translates as "may Christ bless the house."

This longtime tradition is common around the world, especially in Europe, and gaining traction in the United States. I hope the practice continues to grow. The chalking is a simple manifestation—appearance—of our faith. It is another mark that we are followers of Christ, people striving to live in the Way of Love. An echo of the Old Testament, when the Israelites marked their doors to protect them from the plagues, chalking the doors is a tangible reminder of God's grace, love, and protection. Hopefully, the strange equation prompts a quick prayer or recalibration, calling us back to the light, on Epiphany and always.

Richelle Thompson

## Going Deeper

Many churches will bless and distribute chalk during Epiphany. If your congregation doesn't, you might offer to introduce and lead the practice. You can also find a simple prayer for chalking the doors online—or write your own. You might also think about ways you can offer practical gifts to those in need in your community, whether new parents or those who are sick or grieving.

# Epiphany

O God, by the leading of a star you manifested
your only Son to the peoples of the earth:
Lead us, who know you now by faith, to your presence,
where we may see your glory face to face;
through Jesus Christ our Lord,
who lives and reigns with you and the Holy Spirit,
one God, now and for ever. *Amen.*

—*The Book of Common Prayer,* p. 214

I still remember the first time I noticed something about the way we depict and tell the story of Epiphany. Many years ago, I was in a museum with a large collection of medieval Christian art. It was all lovely, and almost all the figures in paintings, statues, icons, and tapestries looked like Europeans. And then I saw a painting of the adoration of the magi. Immediately, I noticed that one of the magi was depicted with dark skin, while the two others had lighter skin.

Curious, I looked around. Suddenly, I could see that this was the convention in many depictions of the magi bringing their gifts to the Christ child.

Later, I learned that this way of portraying the magi is deeply theological. From earliest times, Christians have understood this event, in which pagans traveled a great distance to pay homage, as a manifestation of the truth that Jesus Christ is for all people. He isn't just for a few people in the Holy Land. He isn't just for people of one race. Jesus is for everyone.

It's good for us to remember this. And I hope we'll ask ourselves a follow-up question: are we offering Jesus to everyone, or are we keeping him away from some people? Our task is to tell the Good News of God in Christ to… everyone.

Flipping Epiphany around a bit, we could also place ourselves as the magi in the story. They saw a wondrous sign and traveled a great distance for an uncertain destination for a purpose that might not have been clear to them. Would we be willing to leave our comfortable places to go on a spiritual journey? Would we take risks because we think God is calling us in a new direction?

And, of course, in the end, the magi are given a message in a dream, so they return home by a different way. Are we attentive to the messages and signs that God might be giving us?

So, this Epiphany, let us ask ourselves if we are ready to follow the example of those magi. And let us also ask ourselves if we are ready to be messengers or sign-bearers for others, inviting them to come to adore Jesus Christ. After all, Jesus is for everyone.

Scott Gunn

## Going Deeper

How can you follow the example of the magi? In what ways can you be witness to the light of Christ in your home and community?

# About the Writers

As director of development, **Lindsay Barrett-Adler** loves to connect with the donors who make it possible for Forward Movement to inspire disciples and empower evangelists. Before joining Forward Movement, Lindsay spent ten years as a fundraiser at nonprofits, churches, and schools in Philadelphia. She is a graduate of Capital University and Princeton Theological Seminary. Lindsay and her husband, the Rev. Paul Adler, have three small children and would greatly appreciate more coffee.

**The Rev. Scott Gunn** is executive director of Forward Movement, a discipleship ministry of the Episcopal Church. He travels widely as preacher, speaker, and retreat leader. On Sundays he is not traveling, he serves as priest associate at Christ Church in Glendale, Ohio. Author of several books, his most recent book is *Easter Triumph, Easter Joy: Meditations for the Fifty Days of Eastertide.* Prior to serving at Forward Movement, Scott was a parish priest in the Diocese of Rhode Island. Before that, he had a career in information technology. Scott was educated at Berkeley Divinity School at Yale, Brown University, and Luther College. He lives in Cincinnati with his spouse, the Rev. Sherilyn Pearce.

**Miriam Willard McKenney** is a child of God who fiercely loves her husband, David, and their three adult daughters. She serves as director of mission at Forward Movement and director of dismantling racism for the Diocese of Southern Ohio. She's also a professor of children's literature at Xavier University. Miriam loves to spend time outdoors all year, as nature has gifts to give us every day.

A native of Argentina, **Hugo Olaiz** is an associate editor for Latino/Hispanic resources in Forward Movement. He has a master's degree in Spanish and is an accredited translator. In 2019 he was commissioned by the Episcopal Church to create a new Spanish translation of the Book of Common Prayer. A member of Holy Trinity Church, he lives in Oxford, Ohio, with his husband John-Charles Duffy and a dog named Percy.

For more than 20 years, **Richelle Thompson** has served in the Episcopal Church, committed to sharing stories of faith, discipleship, and innovation. She began her career as a secular journalist, then served as director of communications for the Diocese of Southern Ohio for a decade. Since 2013, Thompson has been managing editor of Forward Movement, where she spearheads content development and production, including *Forward Day by Day*, books, curriculum, and special projects like the Good Book Club and #AdventWord. She lives with her husband, the Rev. Jeffrey Queen, in a slice of God's country Northern Kentucky where the deer feast on the acorns (and some of her flowers), the children walk to school, and the neighbors still wave. They have two young adult children.